HOUSEHOLD TALES OF MOON AND WATER

Poetry by
Nancy Willard

A Harvest/HBJ Book
Harcourt Brace Jovanovich, Publishers
San Diego   New York   London

HOUSEHOLD TALES OF MOON AND WATER

NANCY WILLARD

Library of Congress Cataloging in Publication Data
Willard, Nancy,
Household tales of moon and water.
I. Title.
PS3573-I444H6   1982   811'.54   82-48048
ISBN 0-15-142184-6
ISBN 0-15-642184-4 (Harvest/HBJ: pbk.)
Printed in the United States of America

First Harvest/HBJ edition 1987
A B C D E F G H I J

For Eric

Abril 2, 1989

Gloria:
Se que tu amor por la
poesía y el arte no pude
pensar en algo mejor que
este libro, poético y encantador,
dedicado para una futura
artista.

Espero que cada poema te
inspire.   con cariño

Claudia Liliana H.

This book was completed with the help of grants from the National Endowment for the Arts and from the Creative Artists Public Service Program of New York State.

Our first aim in collecting these stories has been exactness and truth. We have added nothing of our own, have embellished no incident or feature of the story, but have given its substance just as we ourselves received it.

THE BROTHERS GRIMM

Contents

HOUSEHOLD TALES OF MOON AND WATER

Night Light

The moon is not green cheese.
It is china and stands in this room.
It has a ten-watt bulb and a motto:
Made in Japan.

Whey-faced, doll-faced,
it's closed as a tooth
and cold as the dead are cold
till I touch the switch.

Then the moon performs
its one trick:
it turns into a banana.
It warms to its subjects,

it draws us into its light,
just as I knew it would
when I gave ten dollars
to the pale clerk

in the store that sold
everything.
She asked, did I have a car?
She shrouded the moon in tissue

and laid it to rest in a box.
The box did not say *Moon.*
It said *This side up.*
I tucked the moon into my basket

and bicycled into the world.
By the light of the sun

I could not see the
moon under my sack of apples,

moon under slab of salmon,
moon under clean laundry,
under milk its sister
and bread its brother,

moon under meat.
Now supper is eaten.
Now laundry is folded away.
I shake out the old comforters.

My nine cats find their places
and go on dreaming where they left off.
My son snuggles under the heap.
His father loses his way in a book.

It is time to turn on the moon.
It is time to live by a different light.

Vision and Late Supper

Today my son asks me, "What is a vision?"
I say, "Blake saw God in a tree,
and his daddy beat him for telling lies.
That is a vision."

I say, "Your dad saw a ghost ship
passing his vessel
and dropping its cargo of peace.
That is a vision,

and different from having good vision."
I say, "Nero watched the slaughter
of Christians through a ruby
held close to his eye

not for good vision
but for good entertainment."
I take off my glasses.
I say, "Who taught you that word?"

And my son answers, "I saw on TV
a boy like myself.
He held Superman in his hands
and Batman and Falcon and Angel,

and they obeyed him.
Today came a new man, very beautiful.
His name is Vision.
I am saving my money to buy

a Vision." I say,
"If you can buy him
he's not a vision.
Not like your dad, who came to save me

from what some call solitude
and some call grief.
Not like you, thief of our faces
yet wholly your own,

two stars to wish on,
that rise from this table like morning."

Angels in Winter

Mercy is whiter than laundry,
great baskets of it, piled like snowmen.
In the cellar I fold and sort and watch
through a squint in the dirty window
the plain bright snow.

Unlike the earth, snow is neuter.
Unlike the moon, it stays.
It falls, not from grace, but a silence
which nourishes crystals.
My son catches them on his tongue.

Whatever I try to hold perishes.
My son and I lie down in white pastures
of snow and flap like the last survivors
of a species that couldn't adapt to the air.
Jumping free, we look back at

angels, blurred fossils of majesty and justice
from the time when a ladder of angels
joined the house of the snow
to the houses of those whom it covered
with a dangerous blanket or a healing sleep.

As I lift my body from the angel's,
I remember the mad preacher of Indiana
who chose for the site of his kingdom
the footprint of an angel and named the place
New Harmony. Nothing of it survives.

The angels do not look back
to see how their passing changes the earth,

the way I do, watching the snow,
and the waffles our boots print on its unleavened face,
and the nervous alphabet of the pheasant's feet,

and the five-petaled footprint of the cat,
and the shape of snowshoes, white and expensive as tennis,
and the deep ribbons tied and untied by sleds.
I remember the millions who left the earth;
it holds no trace of them,

as it holds of us, tracking through snow,
so tame and defenseless
even the air could kill us.

Questions My Son Asked Me, Answers I Never Gave Him

1. Do gorillas have birthdays?
   Yes. Like the rainbow, they happen.
   Like the air, they are not observed.

2. Do butterflies make a noise?
   The wire in the butterfly's tongue
   hums gold.
   Some men hear butterflies
   even in winter.

3. Are they part of our family?
   They forgot us, who forgot how to fly.

4. Who tied my navel? Did God tie it?
   God made the thread: O man, live forever!
   Man made the knot: enough is enough.

5. If I drop my tooth in the telephone
   will it go through the wires and bite someone's ear?
   I have seen earlobes pierced by a tooth of steel.
   It loves what lasts.
   It does not love flesh.
   It leaves a ring of gold in the wound.

6. If I stand on my head
   will the sleep in my eye roll up into my head?
   Does the dream know its own father?
   Can bread go back to the field of its birth?

7. Can I eat a star?
   Yes, with the mouth of time
   that enjoys everything.

8. Could we Xerox the moon?
   This is the first commandment:
   I am the moon, thy moon.
   Thou shalt have no other moons before thee.

9. Who invented water?
   The hands of the air, that wanted to wash each other.

10. What happens at the end of numbers?
    I see three men running toward a field.
    At the edge of the tall grass, they turn into light.

11. Do the years ever run out?
    God said, I will break time's heart.
    Time ran down like an old phonograph.
    It lay flat as a carpet.
    At rest on its threads, I am learning to fly.

Two Roman Goddesses

First goddess: Deverra

The string broke.
The beads scattered.
I could never collect my wits
if not for you, Deverra,

inventor of brooms.
What worries my feet
is brushed aside.

By moonlight I make
a clean sweep;
ten blue beads,
two pennies,

and a silver pin.
"There is great luck in pins,"
says my mother,

an honest woman
who never lets a pin lie,
not even a crooked one.
"Sweep dust out the door

and you lose your luck,"
says my grandmother,
the unconsecrated Bishop of Dust

and Adviser to Ashes,
herding the lowly together
from dust to dust.
"Don't throw yourself away

on the first man that asks you."
Outside, rain glistens.
I am patient as cats' tongues.

By moonlight I take stock.
Kneeling in dust
at this miniature market,
I pick and choose.

What is lost to sight
is not lost, says the moon,
rinsed clear

as if my mother
rode her broom over it,
lifting the clouds
and letting down

columns of moonlight.
A little temple.
A little night music.

Second goddess: Juno Lucina

By moonlight I see
the anger of shoes,
their laces clenched into knots.

I take the shoes in my lap.
I loosen their tongues.
I take both sides

of the quarrel:
left strand,
right strand.

"When you were born," says my mother,
"the midwife untied
shoes, curtains,

everything."
Nevertheless, I came
with the cord round my neck,

tied like a dog
to my mother's darkness.
The goddess found me.

Her left hand carried the moon,
her right hand lay open like a flower,
empty. Feet first, I followed.

The midwife knocked
breath into me
and knotted that cord for good.

Hush, said the goddess.
Your mother's calling.
You can make it alone now.

For You, Who Didn't Know

At four A.M. I dreamed myself on that beach
where we'll take you after you're born.
I woke in a wave of blood.

Lying in the back seat of a nervous Chevy
I counted the traffic lights, lonely as planets.
Starlings stirred in the robes of Justice

over the Town Hall. Miscarriage of justice,
they sang, while you, my small client,
went curling away like smoke under my ribs.

Kick me! I pleaded. Give me a sign
that you're still there!
Train tracks shook our flesh from our bones.

Behind the hospital rose a tree of heaven.
> *You can learn something from everything,*
> a rabbi told his Hasidim who did not believe it.

> I didn't believe it, either. O rabbi,
> what did you learn on the train to Belsen?
> *That because of one second one can miss everything.*

There are rooms on this earth for emergencies.
A sleepy attendant steals my clothes and my name,
and leaves me among the sinks on an altar of fear.

"Your name. Your name. Sign these papers,
authorizing us in our wisdom to save the child.
Sign here for circumcision. Your faith, your faith."

> O rabbi, what can we learn from the telegraph?
> asked the Hasidim, who did not understand.
> And he answered, *That every word is counted and charged.*

"This is called a dobtone," smiles the doctor.
He greases my belly, stretched like a drum,
and plants a microphone there, like a flag.

A thousand thumping rabbits! Savages clapping for joy!
A heart dancing its name, I'm-here, I'm-here!
The cries of fishes, of stars, the tunings of hair!

> O rabbi, what can we learn from a telephone?
> *My shiksa daughter, your faith, your faith*
> *that what we say here is heard there.*

Nicholas, His Poem

A man and a woman come at midnight
to a white room.
He hangs up their coats.
She puts on a white gown.
She has come to give birth

and he to make you welcome.
The doctor will guard your flesh.
Even the scissors and knives obey him.
Your father will keep your spirit.
Bread and wine are his familiars.

Did you think you could stay whole forever?

For months your mother hid you.
Now it is time to give yourself up.
They put out the light
that the glare of our lives may not
grieve you.

You fall into moonlight.
Wide-eyed and shining, you catch your breath
and rest, meek as a loaf
on your father's hands.
When you enter the warm body

of your first bath
the water greets you,
your mother is weeping for joy,
your father wraps, gathers
you, helpless, traveling by moonlight.

When you are old, you will call this dying.

The Child. The Ring. The Road.

But where are we going? you ask.

To deliver your pain, I answer,
and to make you another.
The first we call sickness,

the second healing.
Why won't you feed me? you ask.
And where are my clothes?

Nobody eats on the way
and you wear what they give you,
I answer, the same for all.

You put on your Cracker Jack ring.
You put on the power
of its ruby-eyed pirate

and his skull-scarred flag.
It is my flag too, I whisper.
How the road shines at night!

One by one you blow out the stars
and now you are counting the doors
to your room, and two women

unfold a gown like a napkin
and truss you into its folds.
Who are those women? you ask.

They are appointed to watch you.
Even at night you are never alone.
I sleep with my eyes open, you say.

They will shut them for you, I answer.
And I slide the ring from your finger
while they wind your body in sails,

sparing only your face, bright cup,
but someone is drinking the light away.
My hand on the shape of your arm,

I walk, you ride, you are the guest.
Good-bye, I say, when we touch the door
which winks to receive you

into its corridors, green, so green;
you have glided into a stem.
Now the lights of that sky have found you.

Now its gardens are sealing your sleep.

Animals Running on a Windy Crown

The music stopped. Everyone clambered aboard.
I was four and fought for the reindeer.
Grandma was seventy-four and chose a goat
without stirrups or saddle.
She lifted me up. Nobody lifted her.
The man in the middle pressed a mirror

and out gushed the "Beer Barrel Polka."
"I always loved that tune," said Grandma,
rising and falling the way she rode
triumphant under the elms downtown
in her old LaSalle after the springs died out.
My steed was swift and unexceptional,

hers wore a ruby in its breast
like Saint Hubert's vision of the stag
when he gave up venison for Jesus.
Beyond her hair haloing in the wind
a Ferris wheel wound up the sun,
its tiny cars ringing the trees to rest.

A Humane Society

If they don't take animals,
I cannot possibly stay at the Statler
no matter how broad the beds
nor how excellent the view.
Not even if the faucets run hot and cold pearls,
not even if the sheets are cloth of gold,

because I never go anywhere without my raccoon,
my blue raccoon in his nifty mask,
the shadow cast by mind over sight.
I never go abroad without consulting his paw
or reading the weather in the whites of his eyes.
I would share my last crust with his wise mouth.

And even if the manager promised
provisions could be made for a blue raccoon,
I cannot possibly stay at the Waldorf,
no matter how many angels feather the fondues,
no matter how many bishops have blessed the soup,
because I never go anywhere without my cat,

my fuchsia cat in her choirboy bow,
in the purity of whose sleep a nun would feel shamed,
in whose dreams the mouse lies down with the elephant.
I never go to bed without setting her at the door
for her sleep robs even the serpent of poison
and no door closes where she takes her rest,

but even if the manager said, very well,
we can accommodate, for a fee, a fuchsia cat,
I cannot possibly stay at the Ritz.
I understand bears are not welcome there.

I understand that everyone walks on two legs,
and I never go anywhere without my bear

who is comelier of gait than any woman,
who wears no shoes and uses no speech
but many a day has laid down his life for me
in this city of purses, assassins, and the poor.
He would give me his coat and walk abroad in his bones,
and he loves a sunny window and a kind face.

I need a simple room papered with voices
and sorrows without circumstance, and an old lady
in the kitchen below who has welcomed
visitors more desperate than ourselves
and who fondly recalls a pregnant woman riding a donkey
and three crazy men whose only map was a star.

Arbor

As a child she planted
these roses, these vines
heavy with trumpets and honey.

Now at the end of her life
she asks for an arbor. At night
she sees roses rooted in heaven,

wisteria hanging its vineyards
over her head, all green things
climbing, climbing.

She wants to walk through this door,
not as she walks to the next
room but to another place

altogether. She will leave her cane
at the door but the door is
necessary. She knows how the raw

space in a wall nearly burned or
newly born makes children pause
and step in. It leads somewhere.

They look out on another country.

No Bees. No Fragrance.

Over your bed at last
comes the stillness of trumpets,

the company of lilies
in small sensible shoes

planted last fall,
worn thin as a hangnail

from standing in place.
They are all mouth, these flowers.

They have nothing to do
with my mouth or my tongue.

They neither hum nor shine.
Rooted in this world

they have grown out of it.
Dear friend, is it this way where you are?

The Sleep of the Painted Ladies

This is my task: to move five cocoons
from an old jam jar to the butterfly cage.

Now they sway from the lid—
five corpses on a gallows

that drop their skins, shrunken to commas
and mark the leaf of their last meal.

I should knock before entering.
This is an ancient place

made for nothing but spinning
and falling asleep.

If I were smaller
or the room larger

I would see an old woman
draw from her outlawed wheel

my hundred years' sleep.
I would hear the snapping of threads,

their cry untuned
at the instant of breaking.

Here lies sleep, sheathed in five copper bullets
I can hold in my hand like aspirin,

five painted ladies who wanted
to travel, to forget everything.

Lightness Remembered

Nor do these heads sing,
though our breath pushes
a blizzard of glass grapes
through the female wand,

a ring of red plastic,
the better
to blow bubbles with.
Through a bowl of soap soup,

the melts of moonlight,
the seduction of sherbet,
my son draws the wand,
and now in the ring shines

a lens
on which he blows
as if he would clean it,
the better to see

the wind with.
O breath, lovely
shaper that makes
a silken windsock,

a nervous tunnel,
a sack soft enough
to hold the unborn,
a glass egg that breaks free

and floats like a planet
over the rose bush,
casting
its rainbow-lipped

shadow on leaves,
on stones—
O wet nose of a spirit,
cold cheek of

the apples of the air,
though he waves the wand,
though he fans you awake,
though you rise again,

there's no saving you.

The Photographer

I

In your darkroom you are a bee.
The drying racks sag with your harvest

of ferns, faces,
the skins of streams,

a nautilus falling asleep. It's you
they dream of, catching their souls

in your black box.
You suffer nothing to be disturbed,

yet you carry, on plates of darkness,
the faces of what loves the light.

Now you shut off your room
against moonlight, against

me. I climb into bed
on the other side of the wall.

All night your radio mumbles.
Anesthetized, wounded, it gives off

loud cries, questions and songs.

II

Today we weeded our garden.
You dig and nothing gets dirty.

I can read your radishes like good typing.
Under my hand the weeds bow down,

they tremble, they tear their leaves.
Mea culpa, I am a milkweed!

Today you photographed the milkweed.
Rejoice, said the field.

You, little brother, are also saved.

The Photographer and the Moon

The moon carries a black box
strapped to her back which she
turns on me.

Still, I leave her my room.
I open the window
and close the door.

When the moon flies in
I hear her running water
and opening her box.

Someone is taking baths,
one after another.
When I take out my dirty

pictures, showing her
self as a new moon,
she stops singing.

I turn my head.
What is that pulse,
that music too far

for the tune to carry,
like a grand ball
on the other side of the water?

The Five Versions of the Icicle

They are the sun's wet nurse, said the mother,
and it milks them to nothing.

They are stockings, said the laundress,
and grievously shrunken.

They are noodles in a broth of diamonds, said the cook,
and they are sausages oiled with light.

They are the parsnips of heaven, said the gardener,
that cannot be grown out of season.

They are the urns of grief, said the widow.
They live on their own tears.

How the Hen Sold Her Eggs to the Stingy Priest

An egg is a grand thing for a journey.

It will make you a small meal on the road
and a shape most serviceable to the hand

for darning socks, and for barter
a purse of gold opens doors anywhere.

If I wished for a world better than this one
I would keep, in an egg till it was wanted,

the gold earth floating on a clear sea.
If I wished for an angel, that would be my way,

the wings in gold waiting to wake,
the feet in gold waiting to walk,

and the heart that no one believed in
beating and beating the gold alive.

Indian Pipe

A twig of pearl breaks
into leaves like the fins
of small fish, the
color of breath in winter.

Indian pipe, they call it.
No man ever smoked
those cartilage flowers,
the first idea of

the first flower, without
color, just as it blew
in the Maker's mind. That's
what it means to be

simple. It feeds on
the dead, leaves rotting
under logs, has its
roots in the sleep

of snails, the souls of
fallen birds, sleep-colored.
Therefore, its clean
skeleton grows bent

under snails' bellies, man's
foot, the breast of the dew,
everywhere present,
everywhere unseen.

Moss

A green sky underfoot:
the skin of moss
holds the footprints of
star-footed birds.

With moss-fingers, with
filigree they line
their nests in the
forks of the trees.

All around, the apples
are falling, the leaves
snap, the sun moves
away from the earth.

Only the moss stays,
decently covers the
roots of things, itself
rooted in silence:

rocks coming alive
underfoot, rain no
man heard fall. Moss,
stand up for us,

the small birds and
the great sun. You know
our trees and apples,
our parrots and women's eyes.

Keep us in your green
body, laid low
and still blossoming
under the snow.

Canna Lily

Pushed out of the earth
like a note in a bottle,

it glistens with joy. A clump
of dirt clasps it still,
the broken seal of

the dead; this green scroll
from some dead sea
flowering.

Fern

Under the dead fronds

stiff as feathers,
the green heads of
the new ferns show
like worms. Blind,

they push up a brace
of umbrellas
offering their handles
of malachite and jade.

Fiddleheads: a
concert for slugs
and snails. We look at
the ostrich fern

and think, not of birds
but of fish spines,
giant tortoises in
the forests turning

to coal, all things
saved by their own
patience: the monstrous
elegance of

their inlaid armor,
the fiddle with no
one to play it,
the fern.

Mushroom

The army retreated and left
under the springs of Queen
Anne's lace and the skin
of cinquefoil, these

tender helmets: *earth star,
cloud's ear, chanterelle,*
mushrooms hunched and hid
like a covey of quail.

The gemmed puffball, gloved
in white kid, darkens
with age like the moon.
"Midwife to the fern and

the great oak, we bear no
flowers, stay nowhere long.
The wind seeds us, shakes
the wheeled loom of our

birth. Haloed in spores,
we lay at your feet our
elf-saddles and friendly
trumpets, unmusical but deep,

having the taste of time sealed
in amphoras and organ pipes:
in the eggs of mythical birds,
the taste of sleep."

Tulip

Innocent as a balloon,
you, tulip, mottle
the plain places.

Snake-backed leaves
or fawn-spotted
like a green animal

from the mind of the
woods, furling its
wings back;

it will presently slip
away. The green
bud seals color like

the eyes of the dead.
But the blood glows
through, as if you

held your heart to
the light. The lips
part, the flower

rolled by hand
opens: a gold-flecked pear
pulses red. Inside,

the pinions engraved
on the petals wear
the quill and shaft

of desire. Speak in a
tapestried tongue.
O creature: speak in fire.

When There Were Trees

I can remember when there were trees,
great tribes of spruces who deckled themselves in light,
beeches buckled in pewter, meeting like Quakers,
the golden birch, all cutwork satin,
courtesan of the mountains; the paper birch
trying all summer to take off its clothes
like the swaddlings of the newborn.

The hands of a sassafras blessed me.
I saw maples fanning the fire in their stars,
heard the coins of the aspens rattling like teeth,
saw cherry trees spraying fountains of light,
smelled the wine my heel pressed from ripe apples,
saw a thousand planets bobbing like bells
on the sleeve of the sycamore, chestnut, and lime.

The ancients knew that a tree is worthy of worship.
A few wise men from their tribes broke through the sky,
climbing past worlds to come and the rising moon
on the patient body of the tree of life,
and brought back the souls of the newly slain,
no bigger than apples, and dressed the tree
as one of themselves and danced.

Even the conquerors of this country
lifted their eyes and found the trees
more comely than gold: *Bright green trees,*
the whole land so green it is pleasure to look on it,
and the greatest wonder to see the diversity.
During that time, I walked among trees,
the most beautiful things I had ever seen.*

* Adapted from the journals of Christopher Columbus, as rendered in William
Carlos Williams' *In the American Grain.*

Watching the shadows of trees, I made peace with mine.
Their forked darkness gave motion to morning light.
Every night the world fell to the shadows,
and every morning came home, the dogwood floating
its petals like moons on a river of air,
the oak kneeling in wood sorrel and fern,
the willow washing its hair in the stream.

And I saw how the logs from the mill floated
downstream, saw otters and turtles that rode them,
and though I heard the saws whine in the woods
I never thought men were stronger than trees.
I never thought those tribes would join their brothers
the buffalo and the whale, the leopard, the seal, the wolf,
and the men of this country who knew how to sing them.

Nothing I ever saw washed off the sins of the world
so well as the first snow dropping on trees.
We shoveled the pond clear and skated under their branches,
our voices muffled in their huge silence.
The trees were always listening to something else.
They didn't hear the beetle with the hollow tooth
grubbing for riches, gnawing for empires, for gold.

Already the trees are a myth,
half gods, half giants in whom nobody believes.
But I am the oldest woman on earth,
and I can remember when there were trees.

The Ceremony of the Coconut

The coconut turns on me
its mummy eyes and
its mummy mouth.

Someone has marked it
for sacrifice:

thrust your awl here.
This is like tapping
a skull, to let out

the headache.
The spirit of pain

leaks away
in oil of silver
and blood of ripe pearls.

Sawed in half,
the coconut proves

its innocence,
its skull
lined with thoughts

so white,
so chaste;

nothing that lives
in the light
can keep that color.

How to Stuff a Pepper

Now, said the cook, I will teach you
how to stuff a pepper with rice.

Take your pepper green, and gently,
for peppers are shy. No matter which side
you approach, it's always the backside.
Perched on green buttocks, the pepper sleeps.
In its silk tights, it dreams
of somersaults and parsley,
of the days when the sexes were one.

Slash open the sleeve
as if you were cutting a paper lantern,
and enter a moon, spilled like a melon,
a fever of pearls,
a conversation of glaciers.
It is a temple built to the worship
of morning light.

I have sat under the great globe
of seeds on the roof of that chamber,
too dazzled to gather the taste I came for.
I have taken the pepper in hand,
smooth and blind, a runt in the rich
evolution of roses and ferns.
You say I have not yet taught you

to stuff a pepper?
Cooking takes time.

Next time we'll consider the rice.

Original Strawberry

The first strawberry:
plain as a teething ring.
And God blessed the strawberry
and eying the future made it
three-leaved for the Trinity
and red for His son's blood.

The strawberry was tasty but sad.
Lord, why make me so low?
And God decreed that the meek
should inherit the earth.

But has a strawberry ears?

On the seventh day it seceded
from creation like a grieving nun.
On the eighth, stars pocked its body
(my sky at sunset, said the strawberry)
and a green sun grew on its north pole
(my vernal equinox, said the strawberry).

Pick a strawberry as if you were paying court.
From which constellation shall you sail
to the mandala
that only a knife can find?

Saint Pumpkin

Somebody's in there.
Somebody's sealed himself up
in this round room,
this hassock upholstered in rind,
this padded cell.
He believes if nothing unbinds him
he'll live forever.

Like our first room
it is dark and crowded.
Hunger knows no tongue
to tell it.
Water is glad there.
In this room with two navels
somebody wants to be born again.

So I unlock the pumpkin.
I carve out the lid
from which the stem raises
a dry handle on a damp world.
Lifting, I pull away
wet webs, vines on which hang
the flat tears of the pumpkin,

like fingernails or the currency
of bats. How the seeds shine,
as if water had put out
hundreds of lanterns.
Hundreds of eyes in the windless wood
gaze peacefully past me,
hacking the thickets,

and now a white dew beads the blade.
Has the saint surrendered
himself to his beard?
Has his beard taken root in his cell?

Saint Pumpkin, pray for me,
because when I looked for you, I found nothing,
because unsealed and unkempt, your tomb rots,
because I gave you a false face
and a light of my own making.

Bones, Scales, etc.

Praise FISH
cold as catacombs,
sign

of light
under the waves
glazing this beach.

Praise *trout*
chained mouth to mouth
on a pine plank.
Grasping the leader
an old man slices

her side as if he were shearing
a breast

and lifts her branchy
spine
from the white sky
that held it.
I hold my son's hand

because a knife splits
the gelatin buttons he
calls *eyes*
and the broken umbrellas
he calls *fins*.

Praise FISH whose beauty feeds us,
and praise MAN who catches the FISH.
Praise also

the knife,
the interpreter.

Wings, Quills, etc.

Dusting the water, a feather
blows like a paper knife
from the swan my son

has been feeding all morning.
Now my son wants to fly
and to nest in the navels of stones

because nothing his body makes
shines so sleek,
grows so bent to its use,

not his hair rinsed with light
or his nails with their small moons rising.
He holds it close like a coin, something saved

to fly with when he is a bird,
to write with when he is a man.

The Generous Body

Body makes things
to give away: milk teeth,
too tiny. It tries again.

Hair also it gives,
strand by strand,
and it charges nothing.

What can be done?
Ruined by losses,
it remembers its mother.

She does not turn her children away!
It arrives at the sea
littered with shells, bones,

and the slow, blind stars.
Into her lap it drops
everything.

Left-handed Poem

Look at your left hand,
clenching the light.

At night it draws pictures
of all it would like

to enjoy, a rock, a face, a flower,
and it heaves them into your sleep

like notes in a bottle:
Open me, read me.

Now look at your right hand,
slower, more gentle,

open for all
it would like to forgive.

Deep in the ovens of sleep,
your left hand is pounding

its terror into loaves,
and your right hand is blessing them.

The Healers

From the print by Helen Siegl

Under your foot at dusk, smell
the compassionate herbs. Their being

is being broken for our need.
Periwinkle, joy of the ground

"maketh a meek stomach and a good heart."
O, caraway in comfits, fennel and seed

of vervain, the simples of grace,
heal us of witchcraft and wagging teeth.

Comforters of the aged and blind,
you make the sinner chaste.

Carried like a staff, you open the dark.
Watchman, what of the night? And you

the servant whose waiting we hardly see:
I am here. Take me.

Being Mended

Crouched on my mending,
my son draws unicorns.

He draws them from life,
not his own at play in

the silence of his work,
or mine tied to my tasks

like spiderwoman. A stitch
in time! I am keeping myself

together. My son draws
on the back of a card marked

You have expired. Time to renew.
My son draws unicorns

as prayers draw angels.
He crumples their heads

like sad cartoons:
So do our prayers appear

to those who receive them.
In the error of his ways

I can almost see
legs slender and strong as the grass,

horns pointing gravely to the stars,
faces human but open

and honest as salt
that spends itself and vanishes.

My son lifts his crayon.
He sits very still.

I drop my sewing
and I go to meet them.

Out of War

In the forest a soldier sees
a child asleep and a fox
rocking the cradle.
The great paws sheathe

blades curved like sickles,
gentle as moths
for rocking. The man waits,
his hand on the new grenades

that he came to throw
in the forest where
no one lives
save a child and a slow

fox with its great claws
curled for catching
small fish and berries
and leaves. They pause,

the fox and his clever
enemy, the man who wants
someone to kill; surely
that would restore whatever

it is he's lost, the weather
of inward mornings, of play
between fox and man's child, of how
they lie down together.

In Praise of ABC

In the beginning were the letters,
wooden, awkward, and everywhere.
Before the Word was the slow scrabble of fire and water.

God bless my son and his wooden letters
who has gone to bed with A in his right hand and Z in his left,
who has walked all day with C in his shoe and said nothing,
who has eaten of his napkin the word Birthday,
and who has filled my house with the broken speech of wizards.

To him the grass makes its gentle sign.
For him the worm letters her gospel truth.
To him the pretzel says, I am the occult
descendant of the first blessed bread
and the lost cuneiform of a grain of wheat.

Kneading bread, I found in my kitchen half an O.
Now I wait for someone to come from far off
holding the other half, saying,
What is broken shall be made whole.
Match half for half; now do you know me again?

Thanks be to God for my house seeded with dark sayings
and my rooms rumpled and badly lit
but richly lettered with the secret raisins of truth.

Family Picnic with Wine and Water

On the banks of a stream,
a Man and a Woman unfold a cloth.

She sets out three goblets
and he sets out a bottle of Saint Père.

She sets out three plates
and he sets the newspaper over his face.

Below the banks where roots
muscle into the water

somebody crouches, half-naked,
picking up pebbles, reading them,

tossing them back to the stream,
somebody small and glad,

the Finder,
the Shining One.

Two Allegorical Figures

Lady, haven't we met before?
Aren't you the baker?
Didn't you take me into your kitchen

and gather the slow sad dough,
too stupid even to breathe,
into white hills, coffins, and domes?

It was you who bustled them into the dark
ovens of great change.
It was I who clapped for the sleepers

vested in crusts of gold,
yet private as beehives and spare
as a hermit's hut.

And that gentleman out in the yard,
the chairman of sacrifice,
he who breaks in horses and doors to rooms

we would never leave if he didn't
carry the walls away: it was he
who broke bread, still warm,

the butter undone at one stroke,
the mild flesh coming alive in our mouths,
honored at last in its own kingdom.

Country Scene

At the desk of the Lamb and Flag sits a Great Dane,
his paw grazing the bell we must touch to wake him.
He shakes himself, he jangles the coins on his neck.
We have arrived at midnight without reservations,
father, mother, son. Even our fear is asleep.

His peaked ears twitch as they gather our names.
For a long time he studies the black book
of all who have certainly stayed and all who might.
Then he asks us in low tones, why have we come?
Did the cock in the kettle crow?

Did a donkey sing?
We shake our heads. No, we heard nothing like that.
In the clock behind him, a sun is rising
like a burnished peach on a perfectly painted tree.
Behind the sun a rabbit is running away,

and behind the rabbit a pack of hounds
flushes the hours out. Eleven! Twelve!
Time passes, stately as deer on the mountain.
The Great Dane listens for yet one more.
But nothing appears, nothing has changed at all.

He waves us to follow him, he has a room that will do,
and he gives us a key fit to open nothing.
It is dotted and crossed, and solid silver.
It waits on my palm like a word
that would light this whole house

if I knew how to say it.

Out of This World I Shall Discover Horses

Once two angels hiding in horses
bore the smoke and the spit of me

over the field of my parents' desire
and bound me into my body, saying:

Your body will grow.
Go the way of the world.
We will never leave you.

So I was born and did not forget them.
Two horses.

Tonight in the twilight
I can't tell

horses from angels. Tonight
what carried me into this world
will carry me out of it.

No-Kings and the Calling of Spirits

The first stringent rule in Ireland was that no one with a
physical blemish could rule as king. The historic King Cormac
was forced to abdicate when he lost an eye.
                    Celtic Mysteries: The Ancient Religion

My cat can look at a king
but can never be
king of his own kind,
this hero of the highway,
spinner
and winner
under the dark wheels.

A real loser:
one eye's stitched over
a dark hole.
One tooth icicles out.
His jaw mended badly.
"On our right we have
Doctor Jekyll,

on our left, Mr. Hyde,"
says my small brother,
who can never be
king of the mountain.
"With his right he'll hear
radios, birds.
With his left, silence,"

says the doctor,
tracing horizons
on a graph designed

to unravel improvement.
I think of losses
graver than his:
lives, limbs, a mind fallen

asleep. I think of the reasons
for giving up
yourself
or a part of yourself,
your eye for an eye,
your arm to an enemy,
your liver and lights

to disease.
I think of wisdom,
its peddlers
and prices.
I think of Odin,
who traded his eye for it
and how only then

did the other eye show him
spirits,
their beauty grazing
the mountains,
their shadows skimming his heart.
At a dark hole my one-eyed cat
worships the invisible mouse.

Small brother,
gifted with silence,
watch over us hunters,
watch over our hands,
our holding on
and our letting go
and our letting go

My Life on the Road with Bread and Water

There was once a woman who loved a river.

African folk tale

I said to BREAD,
Give me something to catch WATER,
a gift that will give him to me forever.

Bread looked into my head
and said Table.
I went home and made Table.
Water set Table,
Water ate his supper,
folded his napkin and went away.

To Bread I said,
Table is useful
but not necessary.

Bread looked into my head
and said Chair.
I went home and made Chair.
Water sat down,
Water stood up,
put out his cigarette and went away.

To Bread I said,
Chair is kind
but not affectionate.

Bread looked into my head
and said Tree.
I went home and made Tree.

Much followed from the making of Tree,
such as roots, bluets,
boars, blue jays, beetles,

worms, etc.
Water lay down in the shade
and later, much later,
chopped down Tree,
burned it all winter
and went away.

To Bread I said,
Tree is patient
but not prudent.

Then Bread looked into my head
and saw emptiness and enormous light.
He breathed on that light
and wrote on that breath: Mirror.

So I went home and made Mirror.
I made this poem, to hold Water.
Who looks for himself will not find it,
and who sees himself will never know who he sees.

Water, I am always bringing you gifts,
loaves to be blessed or suits of fire.
I am sowing myself in your ways like a thistle.

When you wake up, I am your bell.
When you put on your clothes,
you button me to the bone.
When you cut your meat,
it is I you cut, it is I you are eating,
taking me innocently into yourself.

Now I am almost you.
When I open my mouth
I hear your mouth, listening.

Sometimes I am given the gift of Water.

I kneel by Water, my cup in my hands,
and whether I drop it
or whether he takes it, what
does it matter?
In my village when a boat goes down

we say the earth loved it
but Water loved it more
and he is a generous master.
It is himself he gives for our use,
and under my cup as it rides the current

I see his dark face, which he keeps hidden,
I see through one who has nothing to hide.
If I were that cup I would be in good hands.
I would make my home in what travels.
I would not kneel, being equal to everything.

The hands of Water are milk
freckled with stars.

What loves to touch the
wet feet of the mint
does not make houses or
money.

The moon, small enough to spend,
lies on his open palm.
His fingers close over her,
breaking her shell, snap!

When they open, so still, so still,
the moon remembers herself in time.
There she lies, good as new,
sentimental, absurd,

her white heart pulsing
in the terrible hand of Water.

IN WHICH I ASK WATER AN OCCASIONAL QUESTION

Water, when can I give you
this hollow to hold your shadow,
this hill to pillow your head?

Bread says: Wait for the great feasts.
I say: There are not enough of them.

If you leave before I do
what shall I do with your face

which I put on everything?

IN WHICH I MEET WATER FACE TO FACE

I bought a camera
and went to the house of Water.

He showed me his best light.
He put on his white suit.

In my lens he grew still,
a cameo of his former self.

The room being cold, he put on
his dark cloak.

His face, unguarded in the folds
of night,

was the face of a madman
choosing a window,

gathering his body to jump.
My lens is a peephole

through a locked door,
and my hand shakes,

too frightened to press the button.

All night I hear
Water calling

the dead to life.
When the sun goes away,

he does not regret
the passing of light.

Nothing rests in his music,
and everything says farewell.

Water says: I am your dance.
Play me.

Let the deaf lift their heads to listen,
and those to whom feet are not given

rejoice in their roots.
Doesn't every tree hide

the road it unwinds?
Play me.

IN WHICH WATER GIVES ME THE
BOOK OF MY ANCESTORS

Water gave me this book.
It is not written for me.
It is written for birds,

snakes, fishes.
See their bones printed
on limestone.

See this track scratched
on the fresh page of the snow,
leading me into the story.

Someone has gone before me,
cutting the leaves, and now and then
marking a useful passage.

IN WHICH SCRUB BRUSH AND WATER
SPEAK FOR THEMSELVES

Down on my knees in the dirt
I am making my floor
clean
with an old porcupine brush:
scrubba scrubba scrubba.
The radio gossips and soothes.

Half past midnight it
pauses, brings forth
suddenly
the voice of Water,
cracked and broken, flashing
its fins and calling

Come to me! Come to me!
This message was prerecorded
like the light from the stars
that died before you were born.

Meeting Water, I can't speak.
I look at the reeds, the fish.
He looks at the sky.

Time passes, whole schools of it.
When our faces grow still,
we glance at each other.

Then I speak to the reeds
of darkness, to the birds
of miracles, how

living things vanish
into thin air.
After a long time
talk settles down
like silt in the river.
I am calm as honey.

Slowly I pour myself out.
Hello! Hello!
Water shakes my hand.

Hello!
I am so slow
he is already leaving.

Water says: Come to the feast,
and he puts up his banks,
his mud, his black willows,
his sleek rushes.

Mud says: Stop here.
His ways are not your ways.
If he opens his gate,
it is not for you.

Bread, rabbits, stars,
ribbons, lamentations,
all surge forward.
Who is in charge here?

Are we birds
that he feeds us by hand?
or beggars that we
open our fists to be fed?

I wanted something I could carry away,
not this giving which vanishes,
not this quickening
which belongs to no one.

When I enter your house, I bow my head
because even my Lord Fire attends you.
For you, candles lower their mild eyes.
When I sit at your table, I speak with Fire.
I speak of the fire of my youth.
May it burn like a star in my age.
I invoke his heat against winter,
cold feet, and a cold heart.
O, in your service, how the gloss
has gone off him!

Rising to go, I give you my hands
to keep, to remember me by.
You shake your head, *No, no.*
You are too kind.
In my left hand you put
a flagon of ice
and in my right the measure
of Bread which you baked
for me in the ashes of morning,
for the long journey away from you.

IN WHICH WATER TAKES A VACATION

In the summer I look for Water.
I look in his house. I saw him
yesterday, gleaming from room to room.

Now he has rented his rooms to darkness.
Next door the secretary of Water
says to the telephone:

Water is busy. Busy?
Of whom does she speak?
If he is not coming back

I want to lie down in the
small garden in the heart of
the great house, the

last witness of Water.

IN WHICH, BY GOOD LUCK, I LOSE
NEARLY EVERYTHING

Dreaming of Bread, I dreamed of you,
how night after night we wrestled for joy.
Now leaf by leaf you are letting me go.

Some night may I be able to meet
you without hunger,
having forgotten the shine

and the taste of you.

Blessing for Letting Go

I pick up Sad,
I burn it, I scatter the ashes.

Now be thou glad.
Go not with any other woman.
Be curious.
Be beautiful.
Shine.
Life of the earth,
protect this one
who is going to meet you.

Nancy Willard, lecturer at Vassar College and instructor at the
Bread Loaf Writers' Conference, has published short stories,
poetry, and essays, as well as the novel *Things Invisible to See*.
Her award-winning children's books include *The Nightgown
of the Sullen Moon* and *Night Story*. In 1982 she won the
Newbery Medal for *A Visit to William Blake's Inn: Poems for
Innocent and Experienced Travelers*, illustrated by Alice and
Martin Provensen. Nancy Willard lives in Poughkeepsie, New
York, with her husband, Eric Lindbloom, and their son, James.